# The Manifesto and Its Blue Ball

# The Manifesto and Its Blue Ball

Poems by

Llewellyn Mckernan

© 2023 Llewellyn Mckernan. All rights reserved.
This material may not be reproduced in any form, published,
reprinted, recorded, performed, broadcast,
rewritten or redistributed without
the explicit permission of Llewellyn Mckernan.
All such actions are strictly prohibited by law.

Cover photo by Laura Eklund
Cover design by Shay Culligan

ISBN: 978-1-63980-483-2

Kelsay Books
502 South 1040 East, A-119
American Fork, Utah 84003
Kelsaybooks.com

# Acknowledgments

Thank you to the following publications, where versions of these poems previously appeared:

*Artemis:* "Here's the Situation"

*Black Buzzard Revies:* "I Drink Another Bottle of Diet Pepsi"

*Cadence: Florida State Poets Association Anthology:* "This Rain," "Resurrection"

*English Journal:* "First Draft"

*Frgal Chariot:* "If Poetry"

*Grab-A-Nickel:* "How the Mouth Is Created," "The Muse"

*MAW: Magazine of Appalachian Women:* "I Am"

*Revolution Magains:* "A Door"

*Wind:* "The Guest"

"Resurrection" was framed and hung with an exhibit of sculpture and pottery from May 9–31, 1992, in the Boarman Arts Center, Martinsberg, WV.

*The Art of Listening Digital Anthology*: "Whatever Is Worth Listening To"

# Contents

| | |
|---|---|
| Hello | 10 |
| Someone | 12 |
| Here's the Situation | 13 |
| Tree | 14 |
| Whatever Is Worth Listening To | 15 |
| I Drink Another Bottle of Diet Pepsi | 16 |
| Don't | 17 |
| Time Out of Mind | 18 |
| The Horn of My Unicorn | 20 |
| I Believe | 22 |
| This Postmodern Era | 23 |
| You Mean to Say | 24 |
| No, | 26 |
| To the Budding Poet | 28 |
| Haiku | 29 |
| I, Eve, Decree | 30 |
| I swear the trees are talking to me | 31 |
| One October Night | 32 |
| I Decide to Go Fishing | 33 |
| All the Lights | 34 |
| Hey There | 36 |
| The Manifesto | 37 |
| How the Mouth Is Created | 44 |
| The Nose | 45 |
| As for the Ears | 46 |
| The Tongue | 47 |
| I Am | 48 |
| March Wind | 49 |
| A Real Thing | 50 |
| Follow the Leader | 51 |
| The Guest | 53 |
| Possibilities | 55 |
| A Door | 56 |
| This Rain | 58 |
| You Know My Blue Unicorn? | 59 |

| | |
|---|---:|
| My Favorite Day | 60 |
| The Ear | 61 |
| You Are | 62 |
| Take | 63 |
| Ashley Dancing | 64 |
| Edge of Day | 65 |
| First Draft | 66 |
| Mixed Media Presentation | 67 |
| The Tree | 68 |
| The Muse | 69 |
| The Blue Ball | 71 |
| Resurrection | 78 |

# Hello

moon,
skydiving
down a tree, how

about turning
into a smiling,
tipsy-topsy, topsy-turving

bottom lip
of a happy sailor
in the last bar by the everlasting
sea.

# Someone

Reads every word I write,
laughs when I say
"Words bite."

Whispers, "Don't be alarmed.
Every word also
has a leg and an arm."

Tips her hat to the sky when it weeps.
Cradles the sun in her arms
when it falls asleep.

# Here's the Situation

Midnight poetry is called for
Dawn poetry and noon
Poetry of the cat and dog
Frog and loon

Poems you can write on the brim
of a newsboy's hat
A poem that's nothing but the chat
Rain has with a roof

There's music in the opening of a door
Especially if it's old
And the hinges aren't oiled
There's music in a goldfish bowl
that swims around and around
up and down

And then there's the poem
that's only
bound by its own
unearthly
unrehearsed howl, plus
everything
else
in-between—
including a clue (or two)
to
what
cannot be
seen.

# Tree

I count all its branches.
Choose one to sit on.
Eat the night with a spoon.

# Whatever Is Worth Listening To

Listen for areas of sound
Then take your pick and plunge
Into a lake of words that suddenly rise
   and spout
   a staircase spun in air
   a towering fountain
     falling
        falling
          flooding the air
        To somewhere touch the ground
       with you inside it,
drenched
          to the bone
          by a poem.

# I Drink Another Bottle of Diet Pepsi

and go into my usual catatonia

I stiffen a leg
It might as well be an arm
I clench my arm
It might as well be a leg

I squat without bending my back
tie both of my shoes together

I start to get rigid inside my sweater

At this moment the cell phone rings
they call me from Mr. Office

I'm going to stay catatonic I yell
till you give me my walking papers

# Don't

Don't be down-right
right. Take to
a slim blue
world with a wreath
of a corner,
freedom, and
the frog's signature
bubble. Look

for the whiz
of a whistle, the rainbow-
shaped house,
fragrant, ageless
bent-over
by all the brilliant
colors of your
own natural
history.

Undress
the mystery
of summer, savor
the fall's skill-killing
frost, winter's
grid against
the sky, but

love green
spring, angled
to hook the
fish-dreamer.
Eat it whole, though
it's reborn
with each fresh
tick of the clock.

# Time Out of Mind

When I was seven
I was bit by a poem,
I got rabidly
inspired, I barely
survived.

When I was twelve,
and the bell
rang for recess, I
roamed a forest
of books, and
found the neverland
nooks where
meter and
rhyme
hooked me up
just in time,
and ruined my
looks.

When I grew up,
I bit my pencil, and
it bit me back, big-time:
line by line it stung my
thumb and finger,
I wanted to give it
the you know what,
but guess what?
My words flew
across the paper, what
could I do but
turn the hurt into word

after word, darkening
the lead, making
sharper
the point that
matters.

# The Horn of My Unicorn

What color is it?

Black and white,
Gold and ivory.

How did it happen?

The unicorn imagined it
And there it lay
In the meadow,
Wet and sweet.

He picked it up
With his bright blue teeth
And tossed it up
to the sky
(that blessed it twice)
so coming back down,
it found the soot-colored
shaggy beast
ready to meet it more
than half-way—yes,
posed and poised
to juggle it on top
of its pin-striped head, where
the horn spun and
clung so easily, they both
knew it belonged.

What happened then?

The horn
played a spirit-spun song.
The unicorn danced
with heavenly feet and
plunged into a haven
of sweet green trees.

# I Believe

I believe in the violent way.

I believe in the peaceful way, too.

I'd rather believe in nothing,
wear indifference like a sweater
keeping out the cold
that drifts under doors
between the sills of windows.

It's always winter in the Land of Faith
where doubt falls like snow
I gather a handful of

to make a ball which I throw,
to make a snowman the children love.

# This Postmodern Era

These are boring times we're living in
Everyone speaks on the same level
No one is accused of duplicity
For every mystery politics has an answer
All roads lead to China
Lead emission standards are the highest
They've been in a century
Breathing is no longer dangerous
All my friends say nobody is to blame
As if they knew him
Innocent clouds circle a nice blue sky
Scientists launch faultless experiments
Birds nest in Lebanon cedars
It was all perfect to begin with

"What if the music of the spheres
is a constant symphony?"

—Llewellyn McKernan, poet and professor

# You Mean to Say

The universe is just
some concert we're attending?
(The ushers are handing out
  programs, we're dressed to the gills,
  all attention and plumage.)

That raises some questions,
Lady of Light,
I hope you can answer.

Like: Who's conducting?

What are they playing?

Are we the audience?
A musician?
An instrument?

(A bassoon, a brass wind, a fiddle)

You'd be a flute, I bet, or a ukulele.

Or, perhaps, the highest note
on a violin, played only once
in the entire evening.

The note so soft and high
Only the dogs can hear it.

"What if the worst pain is the loss of any explanation for the meaning of life?"

—Llewellyn McKernan, poet and professor

# No,

No, I think that would be
the ultimate happiness. (The moon
reflects the sun, that should be enough,
but it isn't.)

No, the ultimate agony would be
a complete explanation for everything.
Then there would be no more reason
to reason.

No, the ultimate agony would be a
complete explanation for just one thing,
like Danny's suicide, for instance. Then
I would know for certain it could have
been prevented. If only I'd done just
one thing, if only I'd done a thousand.
With that kind of knowledge, I would
die of guilt sooner or later.

No, there is no ultimate agony, they're
all relative, one to the other, one to the
others, others to others, yours to your
brother's brother. That is the ultimate
agony.

# To the Budding Poet

How many times have I told you:

Pray for drought
or flood
Make friends with the bugs
Use the thorns God gave you
Let them grow longer than the rose
So you're done for
No gravy on the table

Remember Blake's advice:
Don't brood twice

You're not better than grass
The perfume your poems give off
When you write, bright and delicate
As the flight of a bird, is nothing
But the nose that smells it

Most important of all:
Get rid of your past
The people who admire you the most
always slash your throat and soak you
in water

Now how in hell
Did those petals open?

# Haiku

Flitter, glitter fire-
fly. Touch-tender little moon,
O, you coldly bloom.

# I, Eve, Decree

That everything begin once
and for all
I'm in love with the earth

The word gives birth
and that's final

that nobody escapes
fecundity: anything goes
there's every reason
to horse around

that's just fine
the way winter has ended
that's just fine
the garden's miraculous
recovery every night
from the darkness among the trees

you make me laugh
you make my skin crawl deliciously
only a madman or a god
loves a goddess like me

to tell you the truth
I don't know what to say
we're standing on the brink
of world peace
and Adam and I are giving
our life for something important

Do you think I'm going to destroy it?

# I swear the trees are talking to me

in the dead of a February winter.
But the longer I listen
the more the consonants and vowels
swirl and whirl, wheel and reel in
a funnel of sound-like words
I never quite get hold of.
I just can't hear what
they have to say.

I haven't learned the language of trees.
I've not met their Teacher.

Perhaps I will someday.

# One October Night

in the depths of sleep
I heard
a caladium leaf
its soft fatal leap

and woke to find
two red feline eyes
on mine

in the night
these bright shiny rocks
had locked within them
all the spinning prisms
Locke called <u>tabula rasa</u>

but if my cat is there
she's nothing
but a grinning Cheshire
I can't find her furry body
anywhere

all night
I dream of cats and prisms

the next day
I find a leaf on the floor

# I Decide to Go Fishing

The first thing I do
when I sit down
to write a poem
is burn my tongue

That's ominous

The saucer is white and shiny china
The cup is blue and shiny, too
And the handle so tiny
 I can easily curl my finger
around it

In a make-believe world I am drinking tea
with Dorothy and the Red Queen and
Porky the Pig

It's a demitasse cup and the coffee is good

But my words are like ashes
For they've burned my tongue

It's numb with anxiety

# All the Lights

in my father's house
are on.
The one in the hall,
The one on the living room ceiling,
The one above the stove means
my mother's cooking.

The radio's playing.
Gene Autry's singing,
"I'm back in the saddle."

I'm stuck in a corner somewhere,
sunk in a vast armchair.
My head's in a puddle,
My back bent
like the bow of an arrow.
The shadow I make
makes the page I'm reading
hazy
the words like gauze.

I'm praying.
To Kafka? Sartre?
Dostoevsky? I'm 32
but my heart's a teenager's.

My father rages.
His roar explodes
like the jet of an old gas heater,
it burns in my ears,
dries up the puddle.

I see the bottom.

My mother's forgotten
to stir the gravy.

Heavens above!
Is this *No Exit*\* on earth?
—the smell

of burnt grease and turkey!

---

\*A play by Jean Paul Sartre where three people are trapped in a room forever.

# Hey There

You there
at the back of my mind

Who are you

I am a tiger ready to spit blood
I am a withered rough-edge bone
I am a star-riddled night

I am  hard  hard  to be born

# The Manifesto

1

Ladies and gentlemen
our first and final word is this:
the poets have begun to write on buses

For the avant-guard
the Long Islanders, the New Yorkers
bus riding's like going slumming
but for us
the people's poets.
it's an absolute necessity.
We couldn't live without buses.

Unlike the former—
and I say this with no respect—
we maintain this:
a bus driver's not like other men
he's not a pharmacist filling
a prescription
a window-washer cleaning a window.

He's an alchemist,
his transfers have cabalistic numbers,
transforming the lead of our steps
into the gold of travel

and one thing more:
he's there
to see we get to our destination.

2

This is our message:
you must learn the names of buses
in the city where you live
the routes they cover:

Cerado-Kenova
West Arlington Heights
Shopping Center
Oak Hills
St. Joseph's Hospital
Third Avenue–Seven Mile
(the one that says In Transit).

All of these—ladies and gentlemen—
must be traveled.
You must inspect the city
scrupulously

like an old woman
inspects the lines on her face
when she looks in the mirror, reading
each new one that takes her deeper into
memories and experiences and history.

3

Waste all your time
and take up space
on the seat of a bus

and somewhere about the city's face:
at the lobe of an ear
the arch of a brow
the edge of a nostril
you'll find yourself one day
sitting pretty.

Words will flow out of your mouth
by chance not meaning
in the latest American fashion
and all for the common people.

A thought isn't born in the heart:
it's born on the steps of a bus.

4

We repudiate:
crawlers
walkers
joggers
airplane riders
train-ticket buyers
hitchhikers
Atlantic city promenaders
front and back seat drivers
bicycles
motorcycles
three-wheelers.

We don't believe in pilots
or muscle exercisers.
Poetry has to be this:
doors that open from the inside out
on rubber springs
or it's absolute rubbish.

5

Well, now on the socio-economic level—
we exchange glances with the other passengers:
a waitress, a cook, a workman,
Alice, Petunia, Porky Pig,
a cop, a thief, a football player—

Refracted instantly in the prism of words
in the end we come out just as we were
just as the bus driver sees us
when he looks in his rear-view mirror.

6

All I know is this:
the bus driver's mouth loves
doughnuts and coffee
jokes and jargon
he exchanges with his regular customers
his belly big and taut
as those in the last stages of pregnancy

who declare themselves in word and deed
for the poetry of birth
the poetry of flesh
the poetry of need.

There is about them
the radiant gray stillness of dawn
just after the darkness has gone
just before the sun arrives.

7

Today I twiddle my thumbs and wonder
why I write about the poetry of the bus

but it's my wanderlust, the blank sky
and the dust I shake off my feet when I

take two steps up—
it's the crow and the crowd of common

speech, the religious chatter, the mean
streak, and the "What's the matter?"

that matters, too.
Then there's the driver, getting balder

by the hour, and the seat up front,
where an infant sprawls, whose mother

is changing its diaper, and me
in the middle row beside the window

where the world looks in to find out what
the real world is doing.

# How the Mouth Is Created

A huge buck
kicks Adam in the jaw

and the wound
lipped and bleeding

takes off

# The Nose

The worm
of death and  its sweet mate
each
with 28 muscles

inch
through the center
of Adam's face
when he's dead  not sleeping

Two nostrils the color
of straw  breathe out
phlegm  and
Adam   resurrected

breathes in
again    the
sweet  stench of skin

## As for the Ears

They were
always here     ahead of us all

even the wind
even the one-celled animals

(whose senses are
one and the same) had them

Leading
to the astounding

but inevitable
conclusion that once the simplest

sense in the universe
was the greatest     Hearing

all things move  in such
harmony   even

the Devil   pumping iron
and mayham and madness   just

played straight
man to God   the sound

coming down to
you and me

one cell
clapping appreciation

# The Tongue

is God's alone

And the Eyes
fresh as a piece

of raw red meat
are not yet done

# I Am

the ripples on a surface
touched with blue plum and

I am a bouquet of crocus
jonquils and Emperor tulips
someone is carrying home

and I am a hummingbird.

At some invisible sign,
I shed my petals, my wings
and leaving behind my past

like a song on the sand I

stand." "Tell me," I say to
the dark gliding in on a leash of long
twilight, zeroing in

on me with such grace and
precision the imminence of
attack seems beautiful. "Tell

me," I cry again, my bird bones
rattling, my hands still webbed
with sand, "Do you dream at night?"

"Do you ever shut your eyes?"

# March Wind

The tree's blue shadow
kneels on the roof of the white-washed

shanty   Smoke gray as the clouds
above it  rears its rhinoceros

mouth up out of a ruined
chimney   The side of the house  in

settling  bends creekward
as your man   tanned   bare-chested  his

arms ballooning like
Mr. America's   pounds nails into the

raw bleeding umber
of new shingles   The bubbly sound of

a banjo dwindles   Something
with a thousand feet starts to walk

from one side the creek
to the other

## A Real Thing

When reflected in water

    say a bright green willow
    leaning over a pond in summer

Is so lucid and lovely—
But don't try to touch it
(or touch it up)

    when you dip your hands in it
    it flees like a bird out of a cage

The cat got its feathers

But in winter
When the pond freezes over
The image is locked tight in its chest
Like jewels

    sparkling emerald lights
    are hidden in a trunk
    white
    cold to the touch
    which no fingers
    fumbling at the lock
    can open

that the first good spell of hot weather

    say in March
    the month that's both lion and lamb

Plunders like a pirate

# Follow the Leader

Jody was it
and I followed

past the barn
where the speckled chicken
with its three eyes
blinked at us
and the birch tree
peeled in the sun

along the path
to the one small brook
on the farm

Jody straddled the air
in a split and run
the carroty cowlick
at the back of his head
glinted and spun

He was it
and I followed

On the stepping stones
we froze like statues
and the minnows rose
and swarmed at our feet
and tweaked the pebbles

In a meadow
we crawled on our bellies
grinding our navels
in grass and bitterweed

what a pass we had come to
how summer burned in our lungs
we lunged like cats
after birdsong
and plunged like deer
into a thicket
where grapevines hung

Jody was it
And I followed

We stopped
and swallowed the air
it burned in our lungs
we undressed
like birch tree bark
peeling in the sun

Jody was it
and I followed

". . . and my eyes, like sherry in the glass the guest leaves."

—Emily Dickinson

# The Guest

The Guest is God. Emily
invites him. He comes

to dinner. What a feast!
She serves him up the truth

about nature, life, human beings.
They break this bread, they

drink this wine together.
He sips the sherry of her

eyes: crème de la crème.
He leaves. At the stroke

of midnight, she's asleep.
No Cinderella, though a

real hearth sweeper. Ash
keeper. God got so drunk

on the vision he slipped
from her veins he staggered

all the way back
to Kingdom Come.

And her? The little
"tippler from Manzanilla"?

Left with the dregs,
she walks on their seas.

# Possibilities

That the sun will set
stroke by stroke.

That the moon will rise
Layered and lovely
as an artichoke.

That petal by petal
I'll pluck the death rose clean.
Nothing left
But pollen

And a bruised pink.

# A Door

You open it
rarely.
Mostly you close it.
Other times you leave a small crack
just enough for the wind
to step through or the sun
to cast shadows.

When you lock it
it's to keep out the dark
or to keep the dark in,
to make time stand still
or leap past the monotonous tick
of the clock.

You strip it
down to one plane, where
a pale gold landscape
gleams, as if
it still holds the rays
of the sun its grains once
soaked up:

Here lines, knots,
whorls call up
the original seasons:
the sky moves
inside the immovable.
The petrified forest
wakes up.

From
behind a tree
a real deer peeps,
its eyes red,
luminous, as if
struck
by car lights, passing
in the dark.

# This Rain

has the voice
of a wild animal, the dazzle

of Picasso, flesh
tender as the inside of a woman's

arm when she's
baking bread in the oven.

With its mushroom
coat, its show-biz patter, its way

of tripping
the light fantastic, it seizes every

thing within
reach, as if it were rifling the vaults

in the Smithsonian
for the Hope Diamond, only to let it

slip through its fingers
at the last moment, so wet and clumsy!

# You Know My Blue Unicorn?

He appears on the white sand
just before it's lifted up into
the bright chaos of a wave.

His diamond-sharp eyes
glance off the rainbow rimming
the china-plate sky, making it burst
into a thousand champagne pieces.

He blinks, his red hoof
stamps the sand as he whips the pale
dream of his mane to whipped cream,
honoring the tide and its hummingbird
rounds, all glittering gutter and green.

Then his ears perk up, as if he hears
a voice just outside this landscape
that makes him so excited
his black tail curls up,
his orange lashes sing.

He neighs, a sound not unlike
goodbye in every language.
He gallops to the edge of the frame,
kicking his hooves high and
with a dazzling soft shoe (that rivals

the best Broadway tap dancer) he exits:
leaving behind his native landscape,
ringing with absence. A bigger
better country called to him.

And he answered.

# My Favorite Day

My Favorite Day is when
nothing happens, when distant hills
soothe up close,
when everything drops
out of my hands but
nothing shatters.

Like today when all my words
rattle the porch swing, even though
I'm not in it, and five wild
roses climb the window sill
as the sun on each wave in the creek

comes into the living room,
which brightens and blinks—This
makes my Baby Grand expand its
black chest, dazzling
the two-time, side-step rhythms
I bang out on the keys—so

all the people I love
who are in a foreign country
start tapping their toes to it—though
each one hears an
entirely different melody—
one that is just

beginning, that is
always just beginning like
my favorite day.

# The Ear

of the unicorn trembles
His hooves

are pink and sweet and
make no sound

when he races in the Kentucky Derby
The hair that grows

down his back is tiger-striped
His teeth are silver   And

when he arrives on
my doorstep for breakfast

turning his profile toward
the sun so it shines like Caesar's

I see his horn
whose music sounds like nothing so much

as a tea-kettle whistle
is invisible

# You Are

the first four notes
in Beethoven's 5$^{th}$ Symphony
the shrill sugar-up
in the vine
the spice of gingerbread
hot from the oven
the hoot owl's cry
a well that's plumb
with a mirror
that shimmers
at the bottom
a branch
loaded with persimmons
orange and sweet
a glass-smooth creek

# Take

Take all the shadows
you've ever made.

Sew them together,
a patchwork of shade—

with buttons of air,
shoulders of cream,

pockets of breath
lined with seems,

a collar and hem
with all that sounds

like the sun rolling back
from every cloud.

A coat made of atoms,
weightless, bare,

a transparency
without wear or tear

Put it on and win
a world you will see

in sparks flying from
earth-warm deeds

taking on the look
of a velvet-soft seed:

the mother of shadows
lying fallow. . .

# Ashley Dancing

Sunlight in her limbs,
stars sparkling in her smallest
gestures,
her long lissome arms
lifted in a hymn
to a gallery of grace, and take
note of that tender
and touching haste, the rolling
splendiferous upside-down
stalk of her hands and feet
that slip and slide her
into the tip-tilted place
where with one carefree capricious
twist of her waist she rises, to leap,
to float, to glide through the air
like silk it eats
as if it were starving

# Edge of Day

The twilight here
is hopeful and hushed.

The air chills
the tiny green lizards

and the toad
on my window sill.

The oak
in the front yard

climbs higher, each
long green leaf

waves to all
the others, the sky

peering through
as if eager to see at last

what's on the ground
before the last of the light

slowly closes all
its doors and windows.

# First Draft

It smiles and smiles
without a face. Rockets

up the tree of an idea,
startling each branch as

it takes on the hue
of heaven, a cap of green

leaves, and the whiskers
of the wind, each jot and

tittle. Its original smile
tucked into the miles

it climbs, up it goes,
growling and spitting

at the idea that grows
as it grows. Teeth sharp

and claws unsheathed,
it creeps out on a limb,

wriggling in and out
of the visible that tunes

its pitch to the metronomic
twitch of a long cat's tail

about to pounce
upon blank:

A Cheshire—
that exits everywhere.

# Mixed Media Presentation

The tree is a green steel
pipe, twisted and cranked

up to speed, each paper bud
ready for a struck match.

The dogwood leaves
are tiny sums, done

in needlepoint, each
tip a Red Cross Knight.

A young girl, hired by
the museum, steps through

the frame, plants herself
beside the tree, one hand

locked around a Knight,
her feet lost in gesso

grass. Her limbs are loose
at the joints, every hair

on her wheat-colored head
is numbered. From where

she stands she can see
the east and its sun,

watches it reach high noon,
sing in evening shadows.

# The Tree

I cannot forget the tree.
Its leaves speak a little French.
Its trunk radiates belief—

Every branch, every
twig does a hey-nonny-
nonny, ding-dong, Do-

little dance, denouncing
the sky, and all its
romantic blue notions

for getting above
the earth to wallow
in wall-to-wall clouds

just to escape the shaking
of the wind that spins
the tree to Kingdom Come

(where it sits in the Garden
till it's overcome) and comes
back again—all its lurking,

alluring roots clawing
black tunnels until they're
buried in solid ground again—

the tree upright as a pole
where a cardinal hides
among its fluffy green cover,

its call twisting like
a rope, deepens
the silence.

# The Muse

If ideas were houses  she
would never visit    if

trees could talk  she
would take up knitting

if art were a leaf
she might be its servant

running up and down
the stairs of the tree

carrying all its white linen
if words were maps

and the ocean
what the seer  sees   she

might with her finger
trace the route from

continent to island  or
delirious from cabin fever

spring on the captain
and crew the brave new world

of hallucinations
coming up out of the blues

with nothing
but the bends to show

for her trouble
But the truth is   truth

can sometimes be seen
budding and dying like

a rose in a garden and
her reveling in all

that goes on in-between:
the angle of the light

(which is also the sum
of all its shadows)

the multitude of weed
the bitter thorn

the rosy whisper that
when it gets petals

speaks in tongues
flaming palely pink

as the sun (that
as it moves into

the dark takes
all of us with it) and

cajoling the wind
that somewhere or other

on this earth
is always blowing

# The Blue Ball

1

shows up
at a poetry reading of sorts
as a balloon
of course

no air escapes
from it   not
even when
the poet tucks poetry
on its string

and up it goes
and how and where
is nobody's business

except there's
a kind of blue ghost
inside each blue syllable
that floats

and whoever listens
looks casually
over its shoulder

2

No fireworks
applaud the blue ball
it can scarcely
be heard   it's too serene
but the words
that spring about when
it bounces and bumps
and lands upon
some glad space and
fills it with grace

make us
clap with our elbows
chirp like birds

what a lark
what a spark
in each curve of a word
that sings

3

O, let us celebrate
the duo of space and time
for the blue ball

of poetry is
here   there   everywhere
present to our presence

from which
it borrows only what
it turns and returns

just in time to move
with the breath's rhythm and
rhyme   each blue

bounce of a sentence
announcing its heaven and horrors
just frees the rest

to keep rumbling and
tumbling coming and going
down to our feet  and up again

following the beat
of good tidings

4

And who keeps the sun
in the sky   who says what
will and what won't go

well   well here's the blue
ball  taking a rest  Its chin scrapes
the floor  the sound scape

grates like a tiny
blue voice  its round fat face
may burst at the point

of a pen but not
when the poet's lips touch the tender
rim of a feeling  that

beams
so grandly true blue
everyone can see it and be seen

5

Who could guess
that it's the poet's voice
that shrinks

to the center
of the blue ball?
Now it can't fall  now

look how it shifts
from one side to another
north  east   south and west

words rumpling and
dumpling inside  dawdling and
daring to land in this hand

or that  or take to his
or her knee   oh how it
changes and cheats and diddles

the same beat  and all
by itself   the refrain it disdains
it shelves on the cuff of some sleeve

as it goes up
and then down and
starts to repeat "A ball will

bounce, but less
and less"  Yes  I think we
would all agree

6

Nothing's ready at all

but the last bounce of the ball

And so it goes

on this whimsical note

to a poetry

of the blues  all shades

and colors     with its

   Azure-wide wonders

    Cobalt kisses

Baby-blue whispers

   Berry-blue snickers

its  Midnight-blue

  blunders with Bright-blue

   traces  and  its Navy-blue aces

      with True-blue graces

that please and ease

Cerulean Sundays   as do

Indigo Mondays with their Royal blue

thunder and Turquoise teasers

and Sapphire secrets!

# Resurrection

                At midnight

in a rented room

on the wrong side of town

        an old man
coughs
            and wakes   coughing

gets out of bed
                    slowly

and with a hand that trembles

   lights a lamp on a table

                picks up a pencil

and a piece of paper

and starts to

                set down

his whole life story

# About the Author

Llewellyn Mckernan grew up writing poetry in a swing on her family's front porch. No skeptic's air there, just a fresh breeze and a nearby shade tree that kept her from being blinded by too much sun.

She grew up well-educated: high school, college, M.A. Degree in English (University of Arkansas), M.A. Degree in Creative Writing (Brown University). But she never really left that front porch swing. It just moved to West Virginia where she wrote poems in the one she found on the porch there, which just fit her lonely lonesome, hoot and holler, heckle-foot state of being.

Now she lives in New Smyrna Beach, Florida, where—though she doesn't have a swing—she has a screened-in back porch where she sits and contemplates the edge of a forest—and still writes poems. And all along, they've gotten published in many journals, including *Artemis, Kalliope, Nimrod, Southern Poetry Review, Antietam Review, Kenyon Review, Now&Then, Appalachian Review,* and *Appalachian Journal*. They've been included in fifty-seven anthologies, and they've won 107 regional, state, or national awards and prizes.

Six of her poetry books have been published: *Short and Simple Annals* (1978, AAUW Author Grant; 2$^{nd}$ ed. 1982, West Virginia Humanities Council Author Grant); *Many Waters* (Mellen Poetry Press, 1993); *Llewellyn McKernan's Greatest Hits* (Pudding House Pres, 2005); *Pencil Memory* (Finishing Line Press, 2010); *The Sound of One Tree Falling* (Motes Books, 2014); and *Getting Ready to Travel* (Finishing Line Press, 2017). She has also had four poetry books published for children: *More Songs of Gladness* (Concordia, 1987); *Bird Alphabet* (Standard Publishing, 1989); *This is the Day* and *This is the Night* (C.R. Gibson, 1994).

She has also been an adjunct English professor at Marshall University (Huntington, WV) and St. Mary's College (Lexington Park, MD) and directed state and regional writing workshops. Her writing mantra comes from the advice that the French novelist Colette gave to a young writer: "Look long and hard at what gives you the most pleasure, but look even longer and harder at what gives you the most pain."

www.ingramcontent.com/pod-product-compliance
Lightning Source LLC
Chambersburg PA
CBHW070939160426
43193CB00011B/1743